To Oz

Thank you so much for your support. Your Spirit, "Say it, See it, Believe it, Receive it."

Love
Deb —

# I AM!
# Say It,
# See It,
# Believe It,
# Receive It.

…the use of positive affirmations

**Created by God**
**Expressed Through Deborah Chenault-Green**

To the memory of my father, James Robert Chenault, Sr., for his strong legacy of music and creativity. To my sister, Janeicer Enez Chenault, whose passion for writing spilled over and lit a flame in my spirit. To my brother, Don Erving Chenault, for teaching us all through his death *to live*. To my brother, James Robert Chenault, Jr. To my grand-son, Terion Farr, for showing us, in his short life, that it doesn't take a long life to touch many lives. And last, but not least, to my heart, my mother, my rock, Elizabeth "Lizzie" Chenault, for teaching me, by example, to be a strong, spiritual, independent, Queen.

*"Create the highest, grandest vision for your life, because you become what you believe.*

**-Oprah Winfrey**

*"Affirmations are a part of my daily routine. Just as I shower, brush my teeth, and eat breakfast every day, I say my affirmations every day."*

**-Diarra Kilpatrick**

*"I believe that I can create. If I can put my head on it right, study it, learn the patterns, it's hard to put into words. It's real metaphysical, esoteric nonsense, but I feel very strongly that we are who we choose to be."*

**-Will Smith**

*"You have to understand; you are a magnet. Whatever you are, that's what you draw to you...if you see it in your mind, you can hold it in your hand."*

**-Steve Harvey**

*"...it's sort of like a mantra. You repeat it to yourself every day. "Music is my life. Music is my life. The fame is inside of me. I'm going to make a number one record and the number one hit." And it's not yet, it's a lie. You're saying a lie over and over and over again, but then one day, the lie is true."*

**-Lady Gaga**

*"…I visualized myself being a famous actor and earning big money. I could feel and taste success. I just knew it would all happen."*

**-Arnold Schwarzenegger**

*"I am not afraid…I was born to do this."*

**-Joan of Arc**

# CONTENTS

# ACKNOWLEDGMENTS

I would like to thank my family for their continued support, encouragement and love in all of my endeavors. To my church family, New Mt. Zion M.B.C., thank you for your support and for keeping me spiritually nourished. To my circle of close friends and "sisters," you have always kept me grounded by keeping it real and loving me unconditionally. There are three people I would especially like to thank: Diarra Kilpatrick, DeEtta West and Donna Marie-Reid, for contributing their touching heartfelt and selfless testimonials. Also, a special thanks to Vanessa Lynn, Sylvia Hubbard-Hutula and Dr. Lisa Biggs for their generous reviews. I am forever grateful. To my son, Melvin Antonio Chenault, thank you so much for your contribution to the book and for starting me on this journey.

# FOREWORD

We live in a world that bombards us with subliminal messaging. From television commercials, to movies and online videos, we can become consumed. Even when we visit a store, we are being manipulated by colors and product placement. We are receiving information and energy that is not of our direct approval or knowing, in most cases. But, there is hope! We can have some measure of control with one of our greatest weapons—our *minds*. Affirmations are a way to stop some of the inner and outer chatter that surrounds and permeates us. We have the power to direct our thoughts to conditions that we find favorable. The great Muhammad Ali was famously quoted for saying, "I am the greatest!" even before he proved it. All of it is energy. So, if you tell yourself something enough times, you *will* become that exact thing. This is true for every facet of your life. Affirmations have the power to change your role from passenger to driver. This book is your driver's manual—except *you* choose the destination and the roads to get there. So, have a fun journey!

*Melvin Antonio Chenault*

*Composer/Classical and Jazz Guitarist*

# PREFACE

*"Death and life are in the power of the tongue."*
(Proverbs 18:21, KJV)

We have been programmed since childhood to speak negativity into our lives, daily. We must understand that words and thoughts are energy and have power. Remember, whatever we put out into the universe will certainly be reciprocated, whether we believe it or not.

## The Law of Perpetual Transmutation of Energy

All persons have within them the power to change the conditions of their lives. Higher vibrations consume and transform lower ones; thus, each of us can change the energies in our lives by understanding the universal laws and applying the principles in such a way as to effect change.

This book has been written as a self-motivating, self-empowering, self-improvement tool and is intended to be utilized continually. I have set it up as a journal, giving the reader a chance to write their own affirmations and take note of the progress that is sure to follow. Affirmations have the power to cancel out anything negative that you may speak or think. Affirmations are not just meant to be read and spoken. They are meant to be repeated as many times as it takes to get the message deep into your spirit and subconscious mind. It is not enough to just read and speak the words. To activate them, you must *believe*. As the Word of God says, "Faith without works is dead." Therefore, you must see yourself being or doing what you affirm (visualization). Then, you must act as if it already is. I am not saying that everything you affirm will come to pass because it still has to be according to God's will and purpose for your life. Just know that when we speak the words, "I am," we are actually saying the name of God because God is the great "I Am." I would even suggest that you end each affirmation with, "In the name of Jesus" because as we know, there is power in the name of Jesus! So, my dear kings and queens, start today to walk into your divine destiny!

# MIND

*"…Truly I tell you, if you have faith as small as a mustard seed, you can say to this mountain, "move from here to there; and it will move. Nothing will be impossible for you."*

**Matthew 17:20 (NIV)**

# Donna Marie-Reid

*Director of Development at East 112th Street
Productions, Beverly Hills, California*

*Donna Marie has been responsible for overseeing the brand's
creative properties and vision, including NBC's Little Big
Shots, Think Like A Man TV Series on FOX, BET's Man
Cave and ABC's Celebrity Family Feud, to name a few.*

*"The only thing that stayed in my mind during this
time was, God didn't bring me this far to leave me.
If I take one step, I know He'll take 10."*

In 2008, I was a producer and in between jobs in the entertainment industry. So, I started working with a staffing agency. They placed me at a TV network as an assistant. Though it was a bit of a "demotion" in position from where I had worked myself up the corporate ladder, I still felt like I hit the jackpot. I felt that way for two reasons: 1) The job came right as I received my last unemployment check; and 2) It was a position at a television network, helping diverse talent get placed on broadcast network shows! What? I would pay *them* to be a part of something so amazing! But I never even considered going this high in the entertainment field. I didn't have any connections there, nor a college degree, both of which you needed to get in. A television network or film studio is the highest level you can go within a corporate structure in entertainment because you get to green light projects.

I got placed into the assignment, made friends with the right people, and worked my butt off! I made myself invaluable to the team so they would have a hard time letting me go. And they did! A two-week assignment turned into a three-month assignment! This could be my new career, I was loving it! Then, I was made aware that they had already chosen a candidate and she was now ready to fill the position. Three months later, I was devastated and a little angry because I was made to believe I had a chance.

Well, instead of setting the newcomer up for a fall, I set her up for success so that she could hit the ground running. I didn't want her first experience at a job so amazing to be a bad one. I helped this unknown person, to my own detriment, because I should have been using the time to set myself up for success by looking for another job. On my last day, the team wanted to take me out to lunch. But I said, "I should stay behind and send out some resumes." After cleaning up my resume and cover letter, I only had time to submit one resume. It was to an anonymous post that read, "Network Executive looking for a creative assistant." By the time I made my submission, my team was coming back from lunch.

Later that night, as I was making dinner, I received a call. They were looking for the person who, "submitted her resume today." With God's grace and mercy, it was the same network I was placed at through the staffing agency, but with even greater opportunity! The network was ABC. I spent eight years there. It was an incredible ride and continues to pay off for me. You don't have to sabotage others to get ahead. God has a plan and a place for us all.

# I am and will always be self-sufficient.

# I am capable of achieving anything that I attempt.

# I am becoming more successful with each passing day.

# I am successful in everything I attempt to accomplish.

# I am immune to lack.

**I am the best at whatever I choose to do.**

**I am a winner; therefore, any and all legal judgment will result in my favor.**

# I am responsible.

# I am able to perform any task put before me.

**I am not the voice of negativity, but the deliverer of positive poetic verse.**

**I am able to exercise discernment in any situation.**

## I am capable of directing both novice actors and the most accomplished actors.

# I am an award-winning playwright and screenwriter.

# I am the writer of great lyrics and melodies.

**I am the author of great works, now and in the future.**

**I am not fearful, of anyone or anything, because
God did not give me the spirit of fear.**

# I choose to forgive past hurts.

**I am endowed with the power of God, and nothing is impossible.**

**I am never going to be detoured from reaching my full potential.**

**I am not swayed by the illusion of fear and doubt.**

# I am creating the world around me.

**I am careful to only focus on the things I**
**want, not the things I don't want.**

**I am not affected by so called problems**
**because I am the solution.**

**I am attracting the right people into my
life, daily, for the right purpose.**

**I am the beneficiary of my Father, in heaven,**
**who is rich in houses and land.**

I am assured that anything I can ever want and need is
already mine. I open my hands and mind to receive it all.

**I am not afraid of success. I relish in it.**

# I am grateful for who I am and where I am.

**I am protected each day from hurt, harm and danger
because God's protective shield cannot be permeated.**

**I am only able to speak to uplift, never to tear down.**

**I am blessed because I am a blessing.**

# I am a blessing because I am blessed.

**I am able to love without prejudice or judgment.**

**I am able to do all things through Christ who strengthens me.**

**I am determined to achieve my every dream.**

**I am determined to receive my every desire.**

**I am drawing nearer to my greatness with each step because my steps are ordered by God.**

**I am not defined by what I have or what I do because these things are transient. If I define myself by these things, how do I define myself when they are gone?**

**I am rich beyond measure because my wealth
is not measured by money alone.**

# I am successful because God says I am.

# I am receiving abundance daily in all areas of my life.

# I am a winner.

**I am ready and willing to receive every
blessing that God has for me.**

**I am never swayed by other people's negative actions.**

# I am the calm in the eye of the storm.

# I am the serenity that I seek.

# I am the embodiment of peace.

# BODY

*…Then He said to her, "Daughter,*
*your faith has healed you."*

**Luke 8:48 (NIV)**

# Deborah Chenault-Green

*Author/Poet/Actress known for: Comedy Central's "Detroiters" (2017, 2018) and Amazon's Pilot show, "The Climb" (2017)*

*"My body is well and whole."*

Affirmations became a daily part of my life in 2002. After receiving a questionable mammogram result, I wallowed in my own pity party. Doctors didn't tell me that I had breast cancer, nor did they tell me that they had found a mass. I was simply told to have another mammogram repeated in six months instead of a year. Well, in my mind, they gave me a death sentence. Within the next couple of hours, in total meltdown mode, I convinced myself I was doomed. I didn't know at the time, but I now know, why God told me to call my son, Melvin. Melvin is the oldest of my four children and he's the only boy. I have three beautiful daughters, Love, Ayana and Maia. But, when it comes to spiritual and philosophical matters, Melvin and I often talk for hours. He has always been a sweet soul and wise beyond his years. He oftentimes spoke about the importance of being positive and speaking positively. He always manages to see the good in all people and all situations.

In my distressed state, he immediately calmed me by reminding me of my faith. He said, "Mom, you have always been a woman of faith and you passed that down to us. Now is the time to exercise that faith." He then said, "The results they gave you, was then. This is now." Melvin, or Deuce as we call him, went on to talk to me about positive affirmations. At the end of that conversation, he gave me some affirmations to use daily. He said, "It's not just about saying them. This is where your faith comes in. It's about believing them." I began speaking the affirmations out loud every day. "My body is well and whole" was one of them. I soon started writing them on sticky notes and placing them on all the mirrors in my house. That way, every time I looked in the mirror, I would be reminded. Well, when I went back for my next mammogram, six months later, the results were favorable. Since then, I have made up my own affirmations for various situations. Today, I am confident that the use of affirmations contributed to me being medication-free from a diabetes diagnosis and in remission, without the use of medicine, for a multiple sclerosis diagnosis in 2003. Not to mention, a recent diagnosis of a Thyroid nodule, which after two months and two biopsies, came back benign. I also attribute affirmations for the complete transformation my life has taken since 2002. Now, I cannot tell you the words to use for the situations you face on a daily basis, but I can share with you some of the ones I have used over the years.

**I am the embodiment of all things positive, pure and nourishing.**

# I am in love with my body.

# I am immune to all forms of arthritis.

**I am immune to all levels of pain.**

# I am immune to gout.

# I am immune to strokes.

# I am immune to multiple sclerosis.

# I am immune to hypertension.

# I am immune to diabetes.

# I am immune to heart disease.

# I am immune to mental illness.

**I am immune to stress.**

_____

_____

_____

_____

_____

_____

_____

_____

_____

_____

_____

_____

_____

_____

_____

_____

_____

# I am immune to sickness.

**I am renewing my mind and body daily.**

**I am healing all infirmity every day.**

**I am strong with the strength of the ancestors.**

**I am imbued with an infinite supply of invigorating energy.**

# I am the example of perfect health.

**I am rebuilding my muscles, continuously, to peak performance and growing stronger in the process.**

**I am regenerating every cell in my body,
every second of every day.**

**I am able to accommodate the flow of blood through my veins, with no obstructions hindering that flow.**

**I am breathing *in* life and breathing *out* infirmity.**

**I am equipped, through God, with an infinite supply of air and oxygen.**

# I am inhaling and exhaling effortlessly.

**I am filling my lungs with limitless amounts
of oxygen with each breath.**

# I am healthy, wealthy and happy.

**I am mentally at ease, knowing that God is a mind regulator.**

**I am built to endure because my strength is limitless.**

**My feet are healthy and they will walk
me into my appointed destiny.**

My hips are strong because they have carried
the weight of the world's gifted.

_____

_____

_____

_____

_____

_____

_____

_____

_____

_____

_____

_____

_____

_____

_____

**My body is whole and it will sustain me through the years.**

# SOUL

*"Therefore I tell you, whatever you ask for in prayer, believe that you have received it, and it will be yours."*

**Mark 11:24 (NIV)**

# DeEtta West

*Actress known for: Rocky (1976); Welcome Home, Roscoe Jenkins (2008); Preacher's Kid (2010); Chandler Christmas Getaway (2018); Saints and Sinners (2018); and Greenleaf (2018).*

Number one: *"The Lord will perfect that which concerns me"* (Psalm 138:8, NKJV). As the Lord set me out on my journey, I always knew that He had His hand on my life. I come from a mother and father who truly loved the Lord—for *real*! They weren't "religious"; they were born-again believers. They brought us up, depositing seeds of love, faith and trust in God into our hearts and spirits. So, on this journey, I had the tools I needed to go and grow. I was not always obedient and patient with the process. As a result, I made some bad choices and decisions. But, along my journey, I would eventually get back on track because He would bring back to my remembrance what He promised in His Word He would do: ...*Perfect that which concerns me.* God has continued to do that every time something arises in my life that throws me off—be it in my marriage, my children, my career, my finances, my health, my ministry and my *life in general.* I reach up and grab that Word and I apply it to my situation. Then, I put my trust in God, knowing that He never fails. He shows His hand every single time that I let Him be in charge.

Number two: *"And we know that all things work together for good for those who love God, to those who are called according to His purpose"* (Romans 8:28, KJV). I love God with all my heart and soul, so this promise certainly applies to me! All that has come and gone in my life has been for a purpose, even those things that didn't feel good. The good, the bad and the ugly! Those things have been working for my good. They will grow me, prune me, restore me, refresh me, remind me, redirect me, strengthen me, preserve me, humble me, instruct me, guide me, heal me and empower me! I have been called for such a time as this to share my story because others need to know that it ain't over until God says it's over. Trust that! It's still working and will continue to work for *your* good if you know your purpose and your calling. If you love God, you have the necessary faith to press forward and keep it moving!

Lastly: *Your latter will be greater than your past.* This was a prophetic word that has been spoken over my life for decades. I received that word from various people around the world. I truly received the word each time it was spoken to me. I remind myself of that daily as I continue to *live*! It has and continues to encourage me as God continues to open so many amazing doors for me. At the age of 69, I am in great health. I am healthier now than I was when I was younger. I'm healthy mentally, emotionally and spiritually. I am comfortable in my skin and I love me. I depend on God daily. He is the one who affirms and validates me. I don't depend on anyone else to do that. When you depend on folks, in most cases, you will be disappointed. They have their own struggles and many of them are comfortable where they are. They don't want to move or they don't have the energy or "know how" to be there for you. I surround myself with people who are not about sucking the life out of me. Folks have challenges, just like I do. But we lift each other up and refuse to attend a "woe is me" party every time the winds of adversity come our way. I am truly blessed and highly favored, walking in victory, not in defeat. Do I feel defeated at times? Yes! But I pick myself up and I know that I am more than a conqueror! I wrote a book years ago entitled, *Get Up!* The tagline is, "Learning how to go through your valley and stand on your mountain." I want to encourage you to keep it moving. Even if it feels a little crazy right now, don't stay in that place of depression, disappointment, discouragement or defeat.

*Get up!* Brush yourself off. Throw your shoulders back and get to steppin'with more boldness and confidence than ever before.

Remember, God will perfect that which concerns you. If you love Him and trust Him, He will work everything out for the good because He already knows that your latter will be greater than your past. Today, you are walking in your *latter*. Don't stop now! There is *greater* coming.

# I am restored by God's grace.

**I am the epitome of God's divine love.**

# I am calm in all situations.

**I am intuitive and I am honing this divine gift, even as I sleep.**

# I am thankful for each moment of my life.

# I am filled with serenity and peace.

# I am in love with me.

**I am open to attract all positive things.**

**I am powerful because God infuses me with His divine power.**

**I am an inspiration to everyone I encounter.**

# I am happy because I deserve to be.

**I am filled with joy each and every morning I wake up.**

**I am my sister's and brother's keeper.**

**I am the apple of God's eye; He loves me beyond measure.**

# I am a friend because I show myself friendly.

# I am the joy that I long for.

**I am forever grateful for God's grace, mercy and favor.**

**I am forever grateful for God's faithfulness.**

**I am wise and I receive more wisdom with each passing day.**

**I am drenched in God's anointing.**

**I am a conduit for the healing light of God.**

**I am a healing tool, infused with the healing light of the Lord.**

# I am a significant being.

# I am a field of infinite possibility.

# I am my true nature: balanced.

I am no longer asleep; I have awakened.

**I am beautiful and my smile radiates from the divine within me.**

**I am the infinite being who God created.**

**I *am*, I have *been*, and I forever *will be*.**

**I am connected to every other soul in the universe; we are one.**

**I am the illumination that forever shines because**
**I am connected to the one and only source.**

**I am the universal donor of an overabundance of love.**

# I am the universal receiver of an overabundance of love.

# I am a peacemaker.

133

**I am capable, willing and able to shine in the company of whomever I encounter.**

**I am the one who holds the keys to a phenomenal future.**

# I am beautiful, desirable and lovable.

**I am able to replace the pain from past hurts with feelings of unconditional love.**

**I am loved beyond measure, and I love immeasurably.**

**I am capable of doing that which Jesus has done and more,**
**for He himself has brought me to this realization.**

# I am cleansed and have been washed as white as snow.

**I am internally and externally in sync
with the flow of the universe.**

**I am grateful for God's favor. It consumes me and reflects outward to those surrounding me.**

# I am able to serve the world with grace and mercy.

**I am God's vessel and I'm ready for Him to pour into me.**

**I am an instrument of the Most High God.**

**I am walking in the assurance of the covering of the blood of Jesus.**

# I am anointed to do God's will.

**I am always positioned to hear from God, who guides me in the direction He wants me to go.**

# I am standing on the promises of God's holy Word.

# I am in God's perfect will.

# I am who God says I am.

**I am who God says I am.**

# My soul is pure and everlasting.

**I am drawing closer to each of my children and grandchildren with each passing day. In the process, our love grows stronger and stronger.**

_____

_____

_____

_____

_____

_____

_____

_____

_____

_____

_____

_____

_____

_____

_____

_____

_____

# I am enough.

**I am a magnet for everything good and positive that life has to offer.**

# AMEN

# ABOUT THE AUTHOR

**DEBORAH CHENAULT-GREEN**, is a Poet, Actress, and Author of "Back 2/1: I Invite You Into My Serenity". As an actress, Ms. Chenault-Green has appeared in numerous stage productions and a plethora of Independent films. Her commercial work has been seen and heard by millions. Sports fans everywhere, my know her from the Henry Ford Hospital commercial, proclaiming, "I have the heart of a champion." She has become known, both nationally and internationally, as "Aunt Lacey," from Comedy Central's hit television series, "Detroiters" and as, "Mrs. Whatsherface," on Amazon's Pilot Show, "The Climb." Her latest film, "Halt," has been nominated for ten awards at The 2019 Detroit Filmmaker Awards.